BOOKS BY LUCILLE CLIFTON

Poetry

Good Times, 1969
Good News About the Earth, 1972
An Ordinary Woman, 1974
Two-Headed Woman, 1980
Next, 1987

Prose

Generations: A Memoir, 1976

Poetry and Prose

Good Woman: Poems and A Memoir 1969-1980, 1987

good woman:
poems and a memoir
1969 – 1980

lucille clifton

BOA Editions, Ltd. ▪ Brockport, NY ▪ 1987

ISBN 0-918526-58-2 Cloth; 0-918526-59-0 Paper

LC number 87-71302

Publications by BOA Editions, Ltd., a not-for-profit corporation under section 501(c)(3) of the United States Internal Revenue Service Code, are made possible in part with the assistance of grants from the Literature Program of the New York State Council on the Arts and the Literature Program of the National Endowment for the Arts, a Federal Agency, as well as grants from private foundations, corporations and individuals.

Designed and typeset at Visual Studies Workshop, Rochester, New York.
BOA logo by Mirko.

Distributed by Bookslinger, 213 E. Fourth Street, St. Paul, Minnesota 55101.

First Edition, 1987

BOA Editions, Ltd.
A. Poulin, Jr., President
92 Park Avenue
Brockport, New York 14420

_____ **contents** _____

good times

good news about the earth

about the earth

heroes

some jesus

an ordinary woman

sisters

i agree with the leaves

two-headed woman

homage to mine

two-headed woman

the light that came to lucille clifton

generations: a memoir

caroline and son

lucy

gene

samuel

thelma

─── good times ───

for maīma

in the inner city
or
like we call it
home
we think a lot about uptown
and the silent nights
and the houses straight as
dead men
and the pastel lights
and we hang on to our no place
happy to be alive
and in the inner city
or
like we call it
home

■

my mama moved among the days
like a dreamwalker in a field;
seemed like what she touched was hers
seemed like what touched her couldn't hold,
she got us almost through the high grass
then seemed like she turned around and ran
right back in
right back on in

■

my daddy's fingers move among the couplers
chipping steel and skin
and if the steel would break
my daddy's fingers might be men again.

my daddy's fingers wait
grotesque as monkey wrenches
wide and full of angles like the couplers
to chip away the mold's imperfections.

but what do my daddy's fingers
know about grace?
what do the couplers know
about being locked together?

■

lane is the pretty one

her veins run mogen david
and her mind just runs.

the best looking colored girl in town
whose eyes are real light brown
frowns into her glass;

I wish I'd stayed in class.

i wish those lovers
had not looked over
your crooked nose
your too wide mouth

dear sister
dear sister   love

■

miss rosie

when i watch you
wrapped up like garbage
sitting, surrounded by the smell
of too old potato peels
or
when i watch you
in your old man's shoes
with the little toe cut out
sitting, waiting for your mind
like next week's grocery
i say
when i watch you
you wet brown bag of a woman
who used to be the best looking gal in georgia
used to be called the Georgia Rose
i stand up
through your destruction
i stand up

■

robert

was born obedient
without questions

did a dance called
picking grapes
sticking his butt out
for pennies

married a master
who whipped his mind
until he died

until he died
the color of his life
was nigger

∎

the 1st

what i remember about that day
is boxes stacked across the walk
and couch springs curling through the air
and drawers and tables balanced on the curb
and us, hollering,
leaping up and around
happy to have a playground;

nothing about the emptied rooms
nothing about the emptied family

■

running across to the lot
in the middle of the cement days
to watch the big boys trembling
as the dice made poets of them
if we remembered to despair
i forget

i forget
while the streetlights were blooming
and the sharp birdcall
of the iceman and his son
and the ointment of the ragman's horse
sang spring
our fathers were dead and
our brothers were dying

■

still
it was nice
when the scissors man come round
running his wheel
rolling his wheel
and the sparks shooting
out in the dark
across the lot
and over to the white folks' section

still
it was nice
in the light of maizie's store
to watch the wheel
and catch the wheel —
fire spinning in the air
and our edges
and our points
sharpening good as anybody's

■

good times

my daddy has paid the rent
and the insurance man is gone
and the lights is back on
and my uncle brud has hit
for one dollar straight
and they is good times
good times
good times

my mama has made bread
and grampaw has come
and everybody is drunk
and dancing in the kitchen
and singing in the kitchen
oh these is good times
good times
good times

oh children think about the
good times

■

if i stand in my window
naked in my own house
and press my breasts
against my windowpane
like black birds pushing against glass
because i am somebody
in a New Thing

and if the man come to stop me
in my own house
naked in my own window
saying i have offended him
i have offended his

Gods

let him watch my black body
push against my own glass
let him discover self
let him run naked through the streets
crying
praying in tongues

∎

stops

they keep coming at me
keep coming at me
all the red lights they got
all the whistles and sirens
blowing with every kind of stop
till i got to go up side a stop
and stop it

even a little old lady
in a liquor store

■

the discoveries of fire

remember
when the skin of your fingers healed
and the smoke rolled away from the
entrance to the cave   how
the rocks cooled down
and you walked back in
once animals and now
men

        ▪

those boys that ran together
at tillman's
and the poolroom
everybody see them now
think it's a shame

everybody see them now
remember they was fine boys

we have some fine black boys

don't it make you want to cry?

■

pity this poor animal
who has never gone beyond
the ape herds gathered around the fires
of europe

all he knows how to do
is huddle with others
in straight haired grunt clusters
to keep warm

and if he has to come out
from the western dirt places
or imitation sun places
and try to make it by himself

he heads, always, for a cave
his mind shivers against the rocks
afraid of the dark
afraid of the cold
afraid to be alone

afraid of the legendary man creature
who is black
and walks on grass
and has no need for fire

■

the white boy

like a man overboard
crying every which way
   is it in your mind
   is it under your clothes
   where oh where is the
   saving thing

    ■

the meeting after the savior gone
4/4/68

what we decided is
you save your own self.
everybody so quiet.
not so much sorry as
resigned.
we was going to try and save you but
now i guess you got to save yourselves
(even if you don't know
   who you are
   where you been
   where you headed

■

for deLawd

people say they have a hard time
understanding how i
go on about my business
playing my ray charles
hollering at the kids—
seem like my afro
cut off in some old image
would show i got a long memory
and i come from a line
of black and going on women
who got used to making it through murdered sons
and who grief kept on pushing
who fried chicken
ironed
swept off the back steps
who grief kept
for their still alive sons
for their sons coming
for their sons gone
just pushing

■

ca'line's prayer

i have got old
in a desert country
i am dry
and black as drought
don't make water
only acid
even dogs won't drink

remember me from wydah
remember the child
running across dahomey
black as ripe papaya
juicy as sweet berries
and set me in the rivers of your glory

Ye Ma Jah

.

if he ask you was i laughing

i wonder what become of my mama
and my littlest girl what couldn't run
and i couldn't carry her
and the baby both
and i took him because he was a man
child
child
pray that the Lord spare hagar
till she explain

■

if something should happen

for instance
if the sea should break
and crash against the decks
and below decks break the cargo
against the sides of the sea
or
if the chains should break
and crash against the decks
and below decks break the sides
of the sea
or
if the seas of cities
should crash against each other
and break the chains
and break the walls holding down the cargo
and break the sides of the seas
and all the waters of the earth wash together
in a rush of breaking
where will the captains run and
to what harbor?

■

generations

people who are going to be
in a few years
bottoms of trees
bear a responsibility to something
besides people
           if it was only
you and me
sharing the consequences
it would be different
it would be just
generations of men
           but
this business of war
these war kinds of things
are erasing those natural
obedient generations
who ignored pride
                  stood on no hind legs
                  begged no water
                  stole no bread
did their own things

and the generations of rice
of coal
of grasshoppers

by their invisibility
denounce us

    ■

love rejected
hurts so much more
than love rejecting;
they act like they don't love their country
no
what it is
is they found out
their country don't love them.

■

tyrone (1)

on this day
the buffalo soldiers
have taken up position
corner of jefferson and sycamore
we will sack the city
    will sink the city
        seek the city

    ■

willie b (1)

mama say
i got no business out here
in the army
cause i ain't but twelve
and my daddy was
a white man

the mother fucker

.

tyrone (2)

the spirit of the buffalo soldiers
is beautiful
how we fight on down to main street
laughing and shouting
we happy together   oh
we turning each other on
in this damn war

■

willie b (2)

why i would bring a wagon into battle
is
a wagon is a help to a soldier
with his bricks
and when he want to rest
also
today is mama's birthday
and i'm gone get her that tv
out of old steinhart's store

■

tyrone (3)

the governor has sent out
jackie robinson
and he has sprinted from center
and crouched low
and caught the ball
(what a shortstop)
and if we buffalo soldiers was sports fans
we sure would cheer

.

willie b (3)

mama say
he was a black hero
a champion like
muhammad ali
but i never heard of it
being not born till 1955

.

tyrone (4)

we made it through the swamps
and we'll make it through the dogs
leaving our white man's names
and white man's traditions
and making some history
and they see the tear gas
burn my buffalo soldiers eyes
they got to say
Look yonder
Tyrone
Is

.

willie b (4)

i'm the one
what burned down the dew drop inn.
yes
the jew do exploit us in his bar
but also
my mama
one time in the dew drop inn
tried for a white man
and if he is on a newspaper
or something
look I am the one what burned down the dew drop inn
everybody say i'm a big boy for my age
me
willie b
son

■

buffalo war

war over
everybody gone home
nobody dead
everybody dying

■

flowers

here we are
running with the weeds
colors exaggerated
pistils wild
embarrassing the calm family flowers   oh
here we are
flourishing for the field
and the name of the place
is Love

■

pork chops
grease stinking out across the field
into the plant where we broke the strike

old man gould sent a train south
picking up niggers
bringing them up no stop
through the polack picket lines
into the plant

chipping like hell
on eight days and off one
sleeping nights between the rows of couplers
hard and stinking out across the field
through the polack picket line
and the strike was broke

lord child i love the union

worked together
slept
fought
in the same town
all the pork chops
fried hard together
stinking together
oh mammy ca'line

a nigger polack ain't shit

■

now my first wife never did come out of her room
until her shoes was buttoned

mama
looked at me and said
you always was a bad boy
and died
gould train come through and
i got on

grampaw's girls was young
could write
their old timey friend was pregnant
and they said they pay my bills
the man was gone
and she was clean as mama

was a girl

never came out of her room
until her shoes was buttoned
scrubbed the wall sometime
twice a day
and i would make her stop   clean
till she died
twenty-one years old

so was grampaw's girl
your mama
i like to marry friends

■

the way it was
working with the polacks
turning into polacks

walked twelve miles into buffalo and
bought a dining room suit

mammy ca'line
walked from new orleans
to virginia
in 1830
seven years old

always said
get what you want
you from dahomey women

first colored man in town
to own a dining room suit
things was changing
new things was coming

you

.

admonitions

boys
i don't promise you nothing
but this
what you pawn
i will redeem
what you steal
i will conceal
my private silence to
your public guilt
is all i got

girls
first time a white man
opens his fly
like a good thing
we'll just laugh
laugh real loud my
black women

children
when they ask you
why is your mama so funny
say
she is a poet
she don't have no sense

■

good news
about the earth

*for the dead
of jackson and
orangeburg
and so on and
so on and on*

_____ about the earth _____

after kent state

only to keep
his little fear
he kills his cities
and his trees
even his children   oh
people
white ways are
the way of death
come into the
black
and live

■

being property once myself
i have a feeling for it,
that's why i can talk
about environment.
what wants to be a tree,
ought to be he can be it.
same thing for other things.
same thing for men.

∎

the way it was

mornings
i got up early
greased my legs
straightened my hair and
walked quietly out
not touching

in the same place
the tree   the lot
the poolroom   deacon moore
everything was stayed

nothing changed
(nothing remained the same)
i walked out quietly
mornings
in the '40s
a nice girl
not touching
trying to be white

■

the lost baby poem

the time i dropped your almost body down
down to meet the waters under the city
and run one with the sewage to the sea
what did i know about waters rushing back
what did i know about drowning
or being drowned

you would have been born into winter
in the year of the disconnected gas
and no car   we would have made the thin
walk over genesee hill into the canada wind
to watch you slip like ice into strangers' hands
you would have fallen naked as snow into winter
if you were here i could tell you these
and some other things

if i am ever less than a mountain
for your definite brothers and sisters
let the rivers pour over my head
let the sea take me for a spiller
of seas   let black men call me stranger
always   for your never named sake

■

later i'll say
i spent my life
loving a great man

later
my life will accuse me
of various treasons

not black enough
too black
eyes closed when they should have been open
eyes open when they should have been closed

will accuse me for unborn babies
and dead trees

later
when i defend again and again
with this love
my life will keep silent
listening to
my body breaking

∎

apology

(to the panthers)

i became a woman
during the old prayers
among the ones who wore
bleaching cream to bed
and all my lessons stayed

i was obedient
but brothers i thank you
for these mannish days

i remember again the wise one
old and telling of suicides
refusing to be slaves

i had forgotten and
brothers i thank you
i praise you
i grieve my whiteful ways

■

lately
everybody i meet
is a poet.

                    "Look here"

said the tall delivery man
who is always drunk

                    "whoever can do better
                    ought to do it. Me,
                    I'm 25 years old
                    and all the white boys
                    my age
                    are younger than me."

so saying
he dropped a six pack
turned into most of my cousins
and left.

    ■

the '70s

will be the days
i go unchildrened
strange women will walk
out my door and in
hiding my daughters
holding my sons
leaving me nursing on my self
again
having lost some
begun much

■

listen children
keep this in the place
you have for keeping
always
keep it all ways

we have never hated black

listen
we have been ashamed
hopeless   tired   mad
but always
all ways
we loved us

we have always loved each other
children   all ways

pass it on

■

driving through new england
by broken barns and pastures
i long for the rains of wydah
and the gardens
ripe as history
oranges and citron
limefruit and african apple
not just this springtime and
these wheatfields
white poets call the past.

■

the news

everything changes   the old
songs click like light bulbs
going off   the faces
of men dying scar the air
the moon becomes the mountain
who would have thought
who would believe
dead things could stumble back
and kill us

■

the bodies broken on
the trail of tears
and the bodies melted
in middle passage
are married to rock and
ocean by now
and the mountains crumbling on
white men
the waters pulling white men down
sing for red dust and black clay
good news about the earth

■

song

sons of slaves and
daughters of masters
all come up from the
ocean together

daughters of slaves and
sons of masters
all ride out on the
empty air

brides and hogs and dogs and babies
close their eyes against the sight

bricks and sticks and diamonds witness
a life of death is the death of life

■

prayer

lighten up

why is your hand
so heavy
on just poor
me?

answer

this is the stuff
i made the heroes
out of
all the saints
and prophets and things
had to come by
this

∎

heroes

africa

home
oh
home
the soul of your
variety
all of my bones
remember

.

i am high on the man called crazy
who has turned nigger into prince
and broken his words on every ear.
he is blinded by the truth.
his nose is sharp with courage.
this crazy man has given his own teeth
to eat devils and out of mine
he has bitten sons.

■

earth

here is where it was dry
when it rained
and also
here
under the same
what was called
tree
it bore varicolored
flowers   children   bees
all this used to be a
place once   all this
was a nice place
once

∎

**for the bird who flew against our window
one morning and broke his natural neck**

my window
is his wall.
in a crash of
birdpride
he breaks the arrogance
of my definitions
and leaves me grounded
in his suicide.

■

God send easter

and we will lace the
jungle on
and step out
brilliant as birds
against the concrete country
feathers waving as we
dance toward jesus
sun reflecting mango
and apple as we
glory in our skin

.

so close
they come so close
to being beautiful
if they had hung on
maybe five more years
we would have been together
for these new things
and for them old niggers
to have come so close   oh
seem like some black people
missed out even more than
all the time

■

**wise: having the ability to perceive and adopt
the best means for accomplishing an end.**

all the best minds
come into wisdom early.
nothing anybody can say
is profound as
no money   no wine.
all the wise men
on the corner.

■

malcolm

nobody mentioned war
but doors were closed
black women shaved their heads
black men rustled in the alleys like leaves
prophets were ambushed as they spoke
and from their holes black eagles flew
screaming through the streets

■

eldridge

the edge
of this
cleaver
this
straight
sharp
single-
handled
man
will not
rust
break, or
be broken

■

to bobby seale

feel free.
like my daddy
always said
jail wasn't made
for dogs
was made for
men

.

for her hiding place
in whiteness
for angela
straightening her hair
to cloud white eyes
for the yellow skin
of angela
and the scholarships
to hide in
for angela
for angela
if we forget our sister
while they have her
let our hair fall
straight on to our backs
like death

■

richard penniman
when his mama and daddy died
put on an apron and long pants
and raised up twelve brothers and sisters
when a whitey asked one of his brothers one time
is little richard a man (or what?)
he replied in perfect understanding
you bet your faggot ass
he is
you bet your dying ass.

■

daddy
12/02 – 5/69

the days have kept on coming,
daddy or not.   the cracks
in the sidewalk turn green
and the Indian women sell pussywillows
on the corner.   nothing remembers.
everything remembers.
in the days where daddy was
there is a space.

my daddy died as he lived,
a confident man.
"I'll go to Heaven," he said,
"Jesus knows me."
when his leg died, he cut it off.
"It's gone," he said, "it's gone
but I'm still here."

what will happen to the days
without you
my baby whispers to me.
the days have kept on coming
and daddy's gone.
he knew.
he must have known and
i comfort my son with the hope
the life in the confident man.

■

poem for my sisters

like he always said
        the things of daddy
        will find him
        leg to leg and
        lung to lung
        and the man who
        killed the bear
        so we could cross the mountain
        will cross it whole
        and holy
"all goodby ain't gone"

    ■

the kind of man he is
for fred

the look of him
the beauty of the man
is in his comings and
his goings from

something is black
in all his instances

he fills
his wife with children and
with things she never knew
so that the sound of him
comes out of her in all directions

his place
is never taken

he is a dark
presence with his friends
and with his enemies
always

which is the thing
which is
the kind of man he is

∎

_____ some jesus _____

adam and eve

the names
of the things
bloom in my mouth

my body opens
into brothers

■

cain

the land of nod
is a desert
on my head   i
plant tears
every morning
my brother
don't rise up

.

moses

i walk on bones
snakes twisting
in my hand
locusts breaking my mouth
an old man
leaving slavery
home is burning in me
like a bush
God got his eye on

■

solomon

i bless the black
skin of the woman
and the black
night turning around her
like a star's bed
and the black
sound of delilah
across his prayers
for they have made me
wise

∎

job

job easy
is the pride
of God

job hard
the pride
of job

i come to rags
like a good baby
to breakfast

■

daniel

i have learned
some few things
like when a man
walk manly
he don't stumble
even in the lion's den

.

jonah

what i remember
is green
in the trees
and the leaves
and the smell of mango
and yams
and if i had a drum
i would send to the brothers
—Be care full of the ocean—

■

john

somebody coming in blackness
like a star
and the world be a great bush
on his head
and his eyes be fire
in the city
and his mouth be true as time

he be calling the people brother
even in the prison
even in the jail

i'm just only a baptist preacher
somebody bigger than me coming
in blackness like a star

■

mary

this kiss
as soft as cotton

over my breasts
all shiny bright

something is in this night
oh Lord have mercy on me

i feel a garden
in my mouth

between my legs
i see a tree

∎

joseph

something about this boy
has spelled my tongue
so even when my fingers tremble
on mary
my mouth cries only
Jesus   Jesus   Jesus

■

the calling of the disciples

some Jesus
has come on me

i throw down my nets
into water he walks

i loose the fish
he feeds to cities

and everybody calls me
an old name

as i follow out
laughing like God's fool
behind this Jesus

■

the raising of lazarus

the dead shall rise again
whoever say
dust must be dust
don't see the trees
smell rain
remember africa
everything that goes
can come
stand up
even the dead shall rise

■

palm sunday

so here come i
home again
and the people glad
giving thanks
glorying in the brother
laying turnips
for the mule to walk on
waving beets
and collards in the air

■

good friday

i rise up above my self
like a fish flying

men will be gods
if they want it

■

easter sunday

while i was in the middle of the night
I saw red stars and black stars
pushed out of the sky by white ones
and i knew as sure as jungle
is the father of the world
i must slide down like a great dipper of stars
and lift men up

■

spring song

the green of Jesus
is breaking the ground
and the sweet
smell of delicious Jesus
is opening the house and
the dance of Jesus music
has hold of the air and
the world is turning
in the body of Jesus and
the future is possible

∎

—— an ordinary —— woman

to fred
you know you know me well

_____ **sisters** _____

in salem

to jeanette

weird sister
the black witches know that
the terror is not in the moon
choreographing the dance of wereladies
and the terror is not in the broom
swinging around to the hum of cat music
nor the wild clock face grinning from the wall,
the terror is in the plain pink
at the window
and the hedges moral as fire
and the plain face of the white woman watching us
as she beats her ordinary bread.

∎

sisters

for elaine philip on her birthday

me and you be sisters.
we be the same.
me and you
coming from the same place.
me and you
be greasing our legs
touching up our edges.
me and you
be scared of rats
be stepping on roaches.
me and you
come running high down purdy street one time
and mama laugh and shake her head at
me and you.
me and you
got babies
got thirty-five
got black
let our hair go back
be loving ourselves
be loving ourselves
be sisters.
only where you sing
i poet.

■

leanna's poem

for leanna webster

one
is never enough for me
you said
surrounded by the lunch
we could not taste for eating,
and i smiled and thought about meals
and mealmates and hunger
and days and time and life and
hunger, and you are right
it is not, it is never enough;
and so this poem is for us,
leanna, two hungry ladies,
and i wish for you
what i wish for myself—
more than one
more than one
more than one.

■

on the birth of bomani
for jaribu and sababu

we have taken the best leaves
and the best roots
and your mama whose skin
is the color of the sun
has opened into a fire and
your daddy whose skin
is the color of the night
has tended it carefully with
his hunter's hands and
here you have come, bomani,
an afrikan treasure-man.
may the art in the love that made you
fill your fingers,
may the love in the art that made you
fill your heart.

∎

salt
for sj and jj

he is as salt
to her,
a strange sweet
a peculiar money
precious and valuable
only to her tribe,
and she is salt
to him,
something that rubs raw
that leaves a tearful taste
but what he will
strain the ocean for and
what he needs.

■

a storm poem

for adrienne

the wind is eating
the world again.
continents spin
on its vigorous tongue
and you adrienne
broken like a bone
should not sink
casual as dinner.
adrienne.
i pronounce your name.
i push your person
into the throat
of this glutton.
for you
let the windmouth burn at last.
for you
let the windteeth break.

■

god's mood

these daughters are bone,
they break.
he wanted stone girls
and boys with branches for arms
that he could lift his life with
and be lifted by.
these sons are bone.

he is tired of years that keep turning into age
and flesh that keeps widening.
he is tired of waiting for his teeth to
bite him and walk away.

he is tired of bone,
it breaks.
he is tired of eve's fancy and
adam's whining ways.

■

new bones

we will wear
new bones again.
we will leave
these rainy days,
break out through
another mouth
into sun and honey time.
worlds buzz over us like bees,
we be splendid in new bones.
other people think they know
how long life is
how strong life is.
we know.

■

harriet
if i be you
let me not forget
to be the pistol
pointed
to be the madwoman
at the rivers edge
warning
be free or die
and isabell
if i be you
let me in my
sojourning
not forget
to ask my brothers
ain't i a woman too
and
grandmother
if i be you
let me not forget to
work hard
trust the Gods
love my children and
wait.

∎

roots

call it our craziness even,
call it anything.
it is the life thing in us
that will not let us die.
even in death's hand
we fold the fingers up
and call them greens and
grow on them,
we hum them and make music.
call it our wildness then,
we are lost from the field
of flowers, we become
a field of flowers.
call it our craziness
our wildness
call it our roots,
it is the light in us
it is the light of us
it is the light, call it
whatever you have to,
call it anything.

■

come home from the movies,
black girls and boys,
the picture be over and the screen
be cold as our neighborhood.
come home from the show,
don't be the show.
take off some flowers and plant them,
pick us some papers and read them,
stop making some babies and raise them.
come home from the movies
black girls and boys,
show our fathers how to walk like men,
they already know how to dance.

■

to ms. ann

i will have to forget
your face
when you watched me breaking
in the fields,
missing my children.

i will have to forget
your face
when you watched me carry
your husband's
stagnant water.

i will have to forget
your face
when you handed me
your house
to make a home,

and you never called me sister
then, you never called me sister
and it has only been forever and
i will have to forget your face.

                        ∎

my boys
for chan and baggy

my boys beauty is
numberless. no kit
can find their colors
in it. only afrikan artists,
studying forever, can
represent them. they are
brothers to each other
and to other live and
lovely things. people
approaching my boys
in their beauty
stand stunned
questioning over and over—
What is the meaning of this?

■

last note to my girls
for sid, rica, gilly and neen

my girls
my girls
my almost me
mellowed in a brown bag
held tight and straining
at the top
like a good lunch
until the bag turned weak and wet
and burst in our honeymoon rooms.
we wiped the mess and
dressed you in our name and
here you are
my girls
my girls
forty quick fingers
reaching for the door.

i command you to be
good runners
to go with grace
go well in the dark and
make for high ground
my dearest girls
my girls
my more than me.

■

a visit to gettysburg

i will
touch stone
yes i will
teach white rock to answer
yes i will
walk in the wake
of the battle sir
while the hills
and the trees
and the guns watch me
a touchstone
and i will rub
"where is my black blood
and black bone?"
and the grounds
and the graves
will throw off they clothes
and touch stone
for this touchstone.

■

monticello

*(history: sally hemmings, slave at monticello,
bore several children with bright red hair)*

God declares no independence.
here come sons
from this black sally
branded with jefferson hair.

■

to a dark moses

you are the one
i am lit for.
come with your rod
that twists
and is a serpent.
i am the bush.
i am burning.
i am not consumed.

■

Kali
queen of fatality, she
determines the destiny
of things. nemesis.
the permanent guest
within ourselves.
woman of warfare,
of the chase, bitch
of blood sacrifice and death.
dread mother. the mystery
ever present in us and
outside us. the
terrible hindu woman God
Kali.
who is black.

■

this morning
(for the girls of eastern high school)

this morning
this morning
           i met myself
coming in

a bright
jungle girl
shining
quick as a snake
a tall
tree girl a
me girl
           i met myself
this morning
coming in

and all day
i have been
a black bell
ringing
i survive
        survive
survive

■

—— i agree with the leaves ——

the lesson of the falling leaves

the leaves believe
such letting go is love
such love is faith
such faith is grace
such grace is god
i agree with the leaves

∎

i am running into a new year
and the old years blow back
like a wind
that i catch in my hair
like strong fingers like
all my old promises and
it will be hard to let go
of what i said to myself
about myself
when i was sixteen and
twentysix and thirtysix
even thirtysix but
i am running into a new year
and i beg what i love and
i leave to forgive me

■

the coming of Kali

it is the black God, Kali,
a woman God and terrible
with her skulls and breasts.
i am one side of your skin,
she sings, softness is the other,
you know you know me well, she sings,
you know you know me well.

running Kali off is hard.
she is persistent with her
black terrible self. she
knows places in my bones
i never sing about but
she knows i know them well.
she knows.
she knows.

∎

she insists on me

i offer my
little sister up. no,
she says, no i want
you fat poet with
dead teeth. she insists
on me. my daughters
promise things, they
pretend to be me but
nothing fools her
nothing moves her and
i end up pleading
woman woman i am trying
to make a living here,
woman woman you are not
welcome in these bones,
woman woman please but she
walks past words and
insists on me.

∎

she understands me

it is all blood and breaking,
blood and breaking. the thing
drops out of its box squalling
into the light. they are both squalling,
animal and cage. her bars lie wet, open
and empty and she has made herself again
out of flesh out of dictionaries,
she is always emptying and it is all
the same wound the same blood the same breaking.

■

she is dreaming

sometimes
the whole world of women
seems a landscape of
red blood and things
that need healing,
the fears all
fears of the flesh;
will it open
or close
will it scar or
keep bleeding
will it live
will it live
will it live and
will he murder it or
marry it.

∎

her love poem

demon, demon, you have dumped me
in the middle of my imagination
and i am dizzy with spinning from
nothing to nothing. it is all your fault
poet, fat man, lover of weak women
and i intend to blame you for it.
i will have you in my head
anyway i can, and it may be love you
or hate you but i will have you
have you have you.

∎

calming Kali

be quiet awful woman,
lonely as hell,
and i will comfort you
when i can
and give you my bones
and my blood to feed on.
gently gently now
awful woman,
i know i am your sister.

■

i am not done yet

as possible as yeast
as imminent as bread
a collection of safe habits
a collection of cares
less certain than i seem
more certain than i was
a changed changer
i continue to continue
where i have been
most of my lives is
where i'm going

.

the poet

i beg my bones to be good but
they keep clicking music and
i spin in the center of myself
a foolish frightful woman
moving my skin against the wind and
tap dancing for my life.

■

turning

turning into my own
turning on in
to my own self
at last
turning out of the
white cage, turning out of the
lady cage
turning at last
on a stem like a black fruit
in my own season
at last

■

my poem

a love person
from love people
out of the afrikan sun
under the sign of cancer.
whoever see my
midnight smile
seeing star apple and
mango from home.
whoever take me for
a negative thing,
his death be on him
like a skin
and his skin
be his heart's revenge.

■

lucy one-eye
she got her mama's ways.
big round roller
can't cook
can't clean
if that's what you want
you got it world.

lucy one-eye
she see the world sideways.
word foolish
she say what she don't want
to say, she don't say
what she want to.

lucy one-eye
she won't walk away
from it.
she'll keep on trying
with her crooked look
and her wrinkled ways,
the darling girl.

∎

if mama
could see
she would see
lucy sprawling
limbs of lucy
decorating the
backs of chairs
lucy hair
holding the mirrors up
that reflect odd
aspects of lucy.

if mama
could hear
she would hear
lucysong rolled in the
corners like lint
exotic webs of lucysighs
long lucy spiders explaining
to obscure gods.

if mama
could talk
she would talk
good girl
good girl
good girl
clean up your room.

■

i was born in a hotel,
a maskmaker.
my bones were knit by
a perilous knife.
my skin turned around
at midnight and
i entered the earth in
a woman jar.
i learned the world all
wormside up
and this is my yes
my strong fingers;
i was born in a bed of
good lessons
and it has made me
wise.

■

light
on my mother's tongue
breaks through her soft
extravagant hip
into life.
lucille
she calls the light,
which was the name
of the grandmother
who waited by the crossroads
in virginia
and shot the whiteman off his horse,
killing the killer of sons.
light breaks from her life
to her lives . . .

mine already is
an afrikan name.

■

cutting greens

curling them around
i hold their bodies in obscene embrace
thinking of everything but kinship.
collards and kale
strain against each strange other
away from my kissmaking hand and
the iron bedpot.
the pot is black,
the cutting board is black,
my hand,
and just for a minute
the greens roll black under the knife,
and the kitchen twists dark on its spine
and i taste in my natural appetite
the bond of live things everywhere.

.

jackie robinson

ran against walls
without breaking.
in night games
was not foul
but, brave as a hit
over whitestone fences,
entered the conquering dark.

■

i went to the valley
but i didn't go to stay

i stand on my father's ground
not breaking.
it holds me up
like a hand my father pushes.
virginia.
i am in virginia,
the magic word
rocked in my father's box
like heaven,
the magic line in my hand. but
where is the afrika in this?

except, the grass is green,
is greener he would say.
and the sky opens a better blue
and in the historical museum
where the slaves
are still hidden away like knives
i find a paper with a name i know.
his name.
their name.
sayles.
the name he loved.

i stand on my father's ground
not breaking.
there is an afrikan in this
and whose ever name it has been,
the blood is mine.

my soul got happy
and i stayed all day.

∎

at last we killed the roaches.
mama and me. she sprayed,
i swept the ceiling and they fell
dying onto our shoulders, in our hair
covering us with red. the tribe was broken,
the cooking pots were ours again
and we were glad, such cleanliness was grace
when i was twelve. only for a few nights,
and then not much, my dreams were blood
my hands were blades and it was murder murder
all over the place.

■

in the evenings

i go through my rooms
like a witch watchman
mad as my mother was for
rattling knobs and
tapping glass. ah, lady,
i can see you now,
our personal nurse,
placing the iron
wrapped in rags
near our cold toes.
you are thawed places and
safe walls to me as i walk
the same sentry,
ironing the winters warm and
shaking locks in the night
like a ghost.

∎

breaklight

light keeps on breaking.
i keep knowing
the language of other nations.
i keep hearing
tree talk
water words
and i keep knowing what they mean.
and light just keeps on breaking.
last night
the fears of my mother came
knocking and when i
opened the door
they tried to explain themselves
and i understood
everything they said.

■

some dreams hang in the air
like smoke. some dreams
get all in your clothes and
be wearing them more than you do and
you be half the time trying to
hold them and half the time
trying to wave them away.
their smell be all over you and
they get to your eyes and
you cry. the fire be gone
and the wood but some dreams
hang in the air like smoke
touching everything.

■

the carver

for fred

sees the man
in the wood and
calls his name and
the man in the wood
breaks through the bark and
the nations of wood call
the carver
Brother

■

let there be new flowering
in the fields let the fields
turn mellow for the men
let the men keep tender
through the time let the time
be wrested from the war
let the war be won
let love be
at the end

∎

the thirty eighth year
of my life,
plain as bread
round as a cake
an ordinary woman.

an ordinary woman.

i had expected to be
smaller than this,
more beautiful,
wiser in afrikan ways,
more confident,
i had expected
more than this.

i will be forty soon.
my mother once was forty.

my mother died at forty four,
a woman of sad countenance
leaving behind a girl
awkward as a stork.
my mother was thick,
her hair was a jungle and
she was very wise
and beautiful
and sad.

i have dreamed dreams
for you mama
more than once.
i have wrapped me
in your skin
and made you live again

more than once.
i have taken the bones you hardened
and built daughters
and they blossom and promise fruit
like afrikan trees.
i am a woman now.
an ordinary woman.

in the thirty eighth
year of my life,
surrounded by life,
a perfect picture of
blackness blessed,
i had not expected this
loneliness.

if it is western,
if it is the final
europe in my mind,
if in the middle of my life
i am turning the final turn
into the shining dark
let me come to it whole
and holy
not afraid
not lonely
out of my mother's life
into my own.
into my own.

i had expected more than this.
i had not expected to be
an ordinary woman.

■

_____ two-headed _____
woman

for elaine and eileen
who listen

———— homage to mine ————

.

lucy and her girls

lucy is the ocean
extended by
her girls
are the river
fed by
lucy
is the sun
reflected through
her girls
are the moon
lighted by
lucy
is the history of
her girls
are the place where
lucy
was going

■

i was born with twelve fingers
like my mother and my daughter.
each of us
born wearing strange black gloves
extra baby fingers hanging over the sides of our cribs and
dipping into the milk.
somebody was afraid we would learn to cast spells
and our wonders were cut off
but they didn't understand
the powerful memory of ghosts.   now
we take what we want
with invisible fingers
and we connect
my dead mother   my live daughter   and me
through our terrible shadowy hands.

.

homage to my hair

when i feel her jump up and dance
i hear the music! my God
i'm talking about my nappy hair!
she is a challenge to your hand
black man,
she is as tasty on your tongue as good greens
black man,
she can touch your mind
with her electric fingers and
the grayer she do get, good God,
the blacker she do be!

■

homage to my hips

these hips are big hips
they need space to
move around in.
they don't fit into little
petty places. these hips
are free hips.
they don't like to be held back.
these hips have never been enslaved,
they go where they want to go
they do what they want to do.
these hips are mighty hips.
these hips are magic hips.
i have known them
to put a spell on a man and
spin him like a top!

■

what the mirror said

listen,
you a wonder.
you a city
of a woman.
you got a geography
of your own.
listen,
somebody need a map
to understand you.
somebody need directions
to move around you.
listen,
woman,
you not a noplace
anonymous
girl;
mister with his hands on you
he got his hands on
some
damn
body!

■

there is a girl inside.
she is randy as a wolf.
she will not walk away
and leave these bones
to an old woman.

she is a green tree
in a forest of kindling.
she is a green girl
in a used poet.

she has waited
patient as a nun
for the second coming,
when she can break through gray hairs
into blossom

and her lovers will harvest
honey and thyme
and the woods will be wild
with the damn wonder of it.

∎

to merle

say skinny manysided tall on the ball
brown downtown woman
last time i saw you was on the corner of
pyramid and sphinx.
ten thousand years have interrupted our conversation
but i have kept most of my words
till you came back.
what i'm trying to say is
i recognize your language and
let me call you sister, sister,
i been waiting for you.

■

august the 12th

for sam

we are two scars on a dead woman's belly
brother, cut from the same knife
you and me. today is your birthday.
where are you? my hair
is crying for her brother.
myself with a mustache
empties the mirror on our mother's table
and all the phones in august wait.
today is your birthday, call us.
tell us where you are,
tell us why you are silent now.

■

on the death of allen's son

a certain man had seven sons.
who can fill the space that
one space makes?
young friend, young enemy who bloomed
off his stick like a miracle
who will he find to fish the waters
he had saved for you?
his name stood at attention
in seven letters,
now there are six
and it never again
can be pronounced the same.

■

speaking of loss

i began with everything;
parents, two extra fingers
a brother to ruin. i was
a rich girl with no money
in a red dress. how did i come
to sit in this house
wearing a name i never heard
until i was a woman? someone has stolen
my parents and hidden my brother.
my extra fingers are cut away.
i am left with plain hands and
nothing to give you but poems.

■

to thelma who worried because i couldn't cook

because no man would taste you
you tried to feed yourself
kneading your body
with your own fists. the beaten thing
rose up like a dough
and burst in the oven of your hunger.
madam, i'm not your gifted girl,
i am a woman and
i know what to do.

■

poem on my fortieth birthday to my mother who died young

well i have almost come to the place where you fell
tripping over a wire at the forty-fourth lap
and i have decided to keep running,
head up, body attentive, fingers
aimed like darts at first prize, so
i might not even watch out for the thin thing
grabbing toward my ankles but
i'm trying for the long one mama,
running like hell and if i fall
i fall.

■

february 13, 1980

twenty-one years of my life you have been
the lost color in my eye. my secret blindness,
all my seeings turned grey with your going.
mother, i have worn your name like a shield.
it has torn but protected me all these years,
now even your absence comes of age.
i put on a dress called woman for this day
but i am not grown away from you
whatever i say.

■

forgiving my father

it is friday. we have come
to the paying of the bills.
all week you have stood in my dreams
like a ghost, asking for more time
but today is payday, payday old man;
my mother's hand opens in her early grave
and i hold it out like a good daughter.

there is no more time for you. there will
never be time enough daddy daddy old lecher
old liar. i wish you were rich so i could take it all
and give the lady what she was due
but you were the son of a needy father,
the father of a needy son;
you gave her all you had
which was nothing. you have already given her
all you had.

you are the pocket that was going to open
and come up empty any friday.
you were each other's bad bargain, not mine.
daddy old pauper   old prisoner,   old dead man
what am i doing here collecting?
you lie side by side in debtors' boxes
and no accounting will open them up.

■

to the unborn and waiting children

i went into my mother as
some souls go into a church,
for the rest only. but there,
even there, from the belly of a
poor woman who could not save herself
i was pushed without my permission
into a tangle of birthdays.
listen, eavesdroppers, there is no such thing
as a bed without affliction;
the bodies all may open wide but
you enter at your own risk.

■

aunt agnes hatcher tells

1. about the war

after the war when rationing was over
was a plenty names. people
shuffled them like cards and drew
new ones out the deck. child,
letters and numbers went
running through whole families.
everybody's cousin was
somebody else. just
consider yourself lucky if
you know who you are.

2. about my mama

your mama, her bottom turned into hamburger
during the war but it was fat meat and
nobody wanted any. she sang Jesus keep me and
beat her fists into fits. fell dead
in the hospital hall
two smiles next to the virgin mary.
glad to be gone.
hunger can kill you.
she's how i know.

3. about my daddy

your daddy, he decided to spread the wealth
as they say, and made another daughter.
just before the war she come calling
looking like his natural blood.
your mama surprised us and opened her heart.
none of his other tricks worked that good.

4. about me

you
slavery time they would be calling you
worth your weight in diamonds the way you
slide out babies like payday from that
billion dollar behind.

■

the once and future dead
who learn they will be white men
weep for their history. we call it
rain.

■

—— two-headed woman ——

in this garden
growing
following strict orders
following the Light
see the sensational
two-headed woman
one face turned outward
one face
swiveling slowly in

∎

the making of poems

the reason why i do it
though i fail and fail
in the giving of true names
is i am adam and his mother
and these failures are my job.

■

new year

lucy
by sam
out of thelma
limps down a ramp
toward the rest of her life.
with too many candles
in her hair
she is a princess of
burning buildings
leaving the year that
tried to consume her.
her hands are bright
as they witch for water
and even her tears cry
fire   fire
but she opens herself
to the risk of flame and
walks toward an ocean
of days.

■

188

sonora desert poem

for lois and richard shelton

1.

the ones who live in the desert,
if you knew them
you would understand everything.
they see it all and
never judge any
just drink the water when
they get the chance.
if i could grow arms on my scars
like them,
if i could learn
the patience they know
i wouldn't apologize for my thorns either
just stand in the desert
and witness.

2. directions for watching the sun set in the desert

come to the landscape that was hidden under the sea.
look in the opposite direction.
reach for the mountain.
the mountain will ignore your hand.
the sun will fall on your back.
the landscape will fade away.
you will think you're alone until a flash
of green incredible light.

3. directions for leaving the desert

push the bones back
under your skin.
finish the water.
they will notice your thorns and
ask you to testify.
turn toward the shade.
smile.
say nothing at all.

■

my friends

no they will not understand
when i throw off my legs and my arms
at your hesitant yes.
when i throw them off and slide
like a marvelous snake toward your bed
your box   whatever you will keep me in
no   they will not understand what can be
so valuable beyond paper dollars diamonds
what is to me worth all appendages.
they will never understand   never approve
of me loving at last where i would
throw it all off to be,
with you   in your small room   limbless
but whole.

■

wife

we are some of us
born for the water.
we begin at once
swimming toward him.
we sight him.
we circle him like a ring.
if he does not drown us we stay.
if he does
we swim like a fish for his brother.

■

i once knew a man

i once knew a man who had wild horses killed.
when he told about it
the words came galloping out of his mouth
and shook themselves and headed off in
every damn direction. his tongue
was wild and wide and spinning when he talked
and the people he looked at closed their eyes
and tore the skins off their backs as they walked away
and stopped eating meat.
there was no holding him once he got started;
he had had wild horses killed one time and
they rode him to his grave.

■

angels

"the angels say they have no wings"

two shining women.
i will not betray you with
public naming
nor celebrate actual birthdays.
you are my two good secrets
lady dark   lady fair.
no one will know that i recognize
the rustle of sky in your voices
and your meticulous absence
of wing.

∎

**conversation with my grandson,
waiting to be conceived**

you will bloom
in a family of flowers.
you are the promise
the Light made to adam,
the love you will grow in
is the garden of our lord.

"and i will be a daisy.
daddy too.
mommy is a dandelion. grandma
you are a flower
that has no name."

∎

the mystery that surely is present
as the underside of the leaf
turning to stare at you quietly
from your hand,
that is the mystery you have not
looked for, and it turns
with a silent shattering of your life
for who knows ever after
the proper position of things
or what is waiting to turn from us
even now?

■

the astrologer predicts at mary's birth

this one lie down on grass.
this one old men will follow
calling mother   mother.
she womb will blossom then die.
this one she hide from evening.
at a certain time when she hear something
it will burn her ear.
at a certain place when she see something
it will break her eye.

■

anna speaks of the childhood of mary her daughter

we rise up early and
we work. work is the medicine
for dreams.
                    that dream
i am having again;
she washed in light,
whole world bowed to its knees,
she on a hill looking up,
face all long tears.
                    and shall i give her up
to dreaming then? i fight this thing.
all day we scrubbing   scrubbing.

                ▪

mary's dream

winged women was saying
"full of grace" and like.
was light beyond sun and words
of a name and a blessing.
winged women to only i.
i joined them, whispering
yes.

.

how he is coming then

like a pot turned on the straw
nuzzled by cows and an old man
dressed like a father. like a loaf
a poor baker sets in the haystack to cool.
like a shepherd who hears in his herding
his mother whisper   my son   my son.

■

holy night

joseph, i afraid of stars,
their brilliant seeing.
so many eyes. such light.
joseph, i cannot still these limbs,
i hands keep moving toward i breasts,
so many stars. so bright.
joseph, is wind burning from east
joseph, i shine, oh joseph,   oh
illuminated night.

■

a song of mary

somewhere it being yesterday.
i a maiden in my mother's house.
the animals silent outside.
is morning.
princes sitting on thrones in the east
studying the incomprehensible heavens.
joseph carving a table somewhere
in another place.
i watching my mother.
i smiling an ordinary smile.

■

island mary

after the all been done and i
one old creature carried on
another creature's back, i wonder
could i have fought these thing?
surrounded by no son of mine save
old men calling mother like in the tale
the astrologer tell, i wonder
could i have walk away when voices
singing in my sleep? i one old woman.
always i seem to worrying now for
another young girl asleep
in the plain evening.
what song around her ear?
what star still choosing?

■

mary   mary astonished by God
on a straw bed circled by beasts
and an old husband. mary marinka
holy woman split by sanctified seed
into mother and mother for ever and ever
we pray for you sister woman shook by the
awe full affection of the saints.

■

for the blind

you will enter morning
without error.
you will stand in a room
where you have never lingered.
you will touch glass.
someone will face you with bones
repeating your bones.
you will feel them in the glass.
your fingers will shine
with recognition,
your eyes will open
with delight.

∎

for the mad

you will be alone at last
in the sanity of your friends.

brilliance will fade away from you
and you will settle in dimmed light.

you will not remember how to mourn
your dying difference.

you will not be better but
they will say you are well.

■

for the lame

happen you will rise,
lift from grounded in a spin
and begin to forget the geography
of fixed things.
happen you will walk past
where you meant to stay,
happen you will wonder at the way
it seemed so marvelous to move.

■

for the mute

they will blow from your mouth one morning
like from a shook bottle
and you will try to keep them for
tomorrow's conversation but
your patience will be broken when the
bottle bursts
and you will spill all of your
extraordinary hearings for there are
too many languages for
one mortal tongue.

■

God waits for the wandering world.
he expects us when we enter,
late or soon.
he will not mind my coming after hours.
his patience is his promise.

■

the light that came to lucille clifton
came in a shift of knowing
when even her fondest sureties
faded away. it was the summer
she understood that she had not understood
and was not mistress even
of her own off eye. then
the man escaped throwing away his tie and
the children grew legs and started walking and
she could see the peril of an
unexamined life.
she closed her eyes, afraid to look for her
authenticity
but the light insists on itself in the world;
a voice from the nondead past started talking,
she closed her ears and it spelled out in her hand
"you might as well answer the door, my child,
  the truth is furiously knocking."

■

———— the light that came ———— to lucille clifton

testament

in the beginning
was the word.

the year of our lord,
amen. i
lucille clifton
hereby testify
that in that room
there was a light
and in that light
there was a voice
and in that voice
there was a sigh
and in that sigh
there was a world.
a world a sigh a voice a light and
i
alone
in a room.

■

incandescence
formless form
and the soft
shuffle of sound

who are these strangers
peopleing this light?

lucille
we are
the Light

■

mother, i am mad.
we should have guessed
a twelve-fingered flower
might break. my knowing
flutters to the ground.

mother i have managed to unlearn
my lessons. i am left
in otherness. mother

someone calling itself Light
has opened my inside.
i am flooded with brilliance
mother,

someone of it is answering to
your name.

∎

perhaps

i am going blind.
my eyes exploding,
seeing more than is there
until they burst into nothing

or going deaf, these sounds
the feathered hum of silence

or going away from my self, the cool
fingers of lace on my skin
the fingers of madness

or perhaps
in the palace of time
our lives are a circular stair
and i am turning

■

explanations

anonymous water can slide under the ground.

the wind can shiver with desire.

this room can settle.

this body can settle.

but can such a sound
cool as a circle
surround and
pray
or promise
or prophesy?

■

friends come

explaining to me that my mind
is the obvious assassin

the terrorist of voices
who has waited
to tell me miraculous lies
all my life. no

i say
friends
the ones who talk to me
their words thin as wire
their chorus fine as crystal
their truth direct as stone,
they are present as air.

they are there.

■

to joan

joan
did you never hear
in the soft rushes of france
merely the whisper of french grass
rubbing against leathern
sounding now like a windsong
now like a man?
did you never wonder
oh fantastical joan,
did you never cry in the sun's face
unreal   unreal? did you never run
villageward
hands pushed out toward your apron?
and just as you knew that your mystery
was broken for all time
did they not fall then
soft as always
into your ear
calling themselves michael
among beloved others?
and you
sister   sister
did you not then sigh
my voices   my voices   of course?

■

confession

father
i am not equal to the faith required.
i doubt.
i have a woman's certainties;
bodies pulled from me,
pushed into me.
bone flesh is what i know.

father
the angels say they have no wings.
i woke one morning
feeling how to see them.
i could discern their shadows
in the shadow. i am not
equal to the faith required.

father
i see your mother standing now
shoulderless and shoeless by your side.
i hear her whisper truths i cannot know.
father i doubt.

father
what are the actual certainties?
your mother speaks of love.

the angels say they have no wings.
i am not equal to the faith required.
i try to run from such surprising presence;
the angels stream before me
like a torch.

∎

in populated air
our ancestors continue.
i have seen them.
i have heard
their shimmering voices
singing.

.

—— generations: ——
a memoir

*Lo, mine eye hath seen all this, mine ear hath heard and understood it.
What ye know, the same do I know also; I am not inferior unto you.*

—Job 13:1 and 2

Get what you want, you from Dahomey women.

—The woman called Caroline Donald Sale
born free in Afrika in 1822
died free in America in 1910

_____ caroline and son _____

I celebrate myself, and sing myself,
And what I assume you shall assume,
For every atom belonging to me as good belongs to you.

—Song of Myself
Walt Whitman

1

She said

I saw your notice in the Bedford newspaper and I thought isn't this interesting, so I figured I would call you and tell you that I am a Sale and I have compiled and privately printed a history of the Sale/Sayle family of Bedford County Virginia and I would be glad to send it to you. But why are you interested in the Sayles?

Her voice is sweet and white over the wires. What shall I say to this white lady? What does it matter now that Daddy is dead and I am a Clifton?

Have you ever heard of a man named John F. Sale? I ask.

Why yes, he was a great-uncle of mine, I believe. She is happy and excited.

Well, my maiden name was Sayles, I say.

What was your father's name? she asks. She is jumping through the wires.

Samuel, I say.

She is puzzled. I don't remember that name, she says.

Who remembers the names of the slaves? Only the children of slaves. The names are Caroline and Lucy and Samuel, I say. Slave names.

Ooooh, she cries. Oh that's just awful. And there is silence.

Then she tells me that the slave cabins are still there at the Sale home where she lives, and the graves of the slaves are there, unmarked. The graves of my family. She remembers the name Caroline, she says, her parents were delivered by the midwife, Mammy Caroline. The midwife Mammy Caroline.

Is the Nichols house still there? I ask.

Still with the family in it, she says. I hear the trouble in her voice.

And I rush to reassure her. Why? Is it in my blood to reassure this thin-voiced white lady? I am a Clifton now, I say. I only wanted to find out about these things. I am only curious, I say. It's a long time after, and I just wanted to know.

I can help you, she sighs. I can help you.

But I never hear her voice again.

Yet she sends the history she has compiled and in it are her family's names. And our family names are thick in her family like an omen. I see that she is the last of her line. Old and not married, left with a house and a name. I look at my husband and our six children and I feel the Dahomey women gathering in my bones.

"They called her Ca'line," Daddy would tell us. "What her African name was, I never heard her say. I asked her one time to tell me and she just shook her head. But it'll be forgot, I hollered at her, it'll be forgot. She just smiled at me and said 'Don't you worry, mister, don't you worry.'"

■

2

She said
　he finished his eggs and his bacon and his coffee and said Jo get me one of them True Greens and I got him his cigarette and went upstairs to get a ashtray and when I got back he was laying on the floor and blood was all on his mouth like when Mama used to have her fits and I hollered Daddy Daddy Daddy and Bobby come running down the stairs to see what was the matter and when he saw he called the rescue squad but when they got here they said he was dead. I didn't believe it.

Punkin calling from Buffalo, talking soft and slow like she did when she was high. Lue, Lue, Daddy is dead.

I didn't believe her. I hung up the phone and went back to reading the paper and waited for Fred and Sammy to come back home. I didn't believe Mr. Sayles Lord was dead. I didn't believe Old Brother Sayles was dead. I didn't believe the Rock was dead. I didn't believe you were dead Daddy. You said you stayed on here because we had feet of clay. I didn't believe you could die Daddy. I didn't believe you would. I didn't want you to die Daddy. You always said you would haunt us if you did.

We drove North, seeing everything and laughing the whole way. Miss Mattie came and got the kids and I stopped by Sears and bought a black hat and Fred and Sammy got a map and we headed North, Fred driving.

Mammy Ca'line walked North from New Orleans to Virginia in 1830. She was eight years old.

　■

3

"Mammy Ca'line raised me," Daddy would say. "After my Grandma Lucy died, she took care of Genie and then took care of me. She was my great-grandmother, Lucy's Mama, you know, but everybody called her Mammy like they did in them days. Oh she was tall and skinny and walked straight as a soldier, Lue. Straight like somebody marching wherever she went. And she talked with a Oxford accent! I ain't kidding. Don't let nobody tell you them old people was dumb. She talked like she was from London England and when we kids would be running and hooping and hollering all around she would come to the door and look straight at me and shake her finger and say 'Stop that Bedlam, mister, stop that Bedlam, I say.' With a Oxford accent, Lue! She was a dark old skinny lady and she raised my Daddy and then raised me, least till I was eight years old when she died. When I was eight years old. I remember everything she ever told me, cause you know when you that age you old enough to remember things. I remember everything she told me, Lue, even though she died when I was eight years old. And then I knowed about what she remembered cause that's how old she was when she got here. Eight years old."

■

4

Driving out of Baltimore you turn around narrow one-way streets and long-named alleys and stop in lines of schoolteachers on Monday mornings. Every car had a woman driver except ours.

Where are the men, I laughed. On the corners, Sammy laughed back. Everything was funny. Everything was funny. We curved and crawled around past Ward's, past the last hamburger before the highway and broke out of the city like out of chains. Fred gunned the motor and laughed and we left Baltimore behind us. An old Black lady watched us making noise outside her country door. I could hear her head shaking. This is Maryland farm country, we be nice niggers here. I laughed at her frown. Fred nodded his head toward the front of the car. Be careful, he said, Pennsylvania is out there. We all laughed. Everything was funny.

"Walking from New Orleans to Virginia," Daddy would say, "you go through Mississippi, Alabama, Georgia, South Carolina and North Carolina. And that's the walk Mammy Ca'line took when she was eight years old. She was born among the Dahomey people in 1822, Lue. Among the Dahomey people, and she used to always say 'Get what you want, you from Dahomey women.' And she used to tell us about how they had a whole army of nothing but women back there and how they was the best soldiers in the world. And she was from among the Dahomey people and one day her and her Mama and her sister and her brother was captured and throwed on a boat and on a boat till they landed in New Orleans. And I would ask her how did you get captured, Mammy, and she would say that she was a child and I would ask her when did it happen, Mammy, and she would say 'In 1830 I walked from New Orleans to Virginia and I was eight years old.' And I would ask her what was it like on the boat and she would just shake her head. And it seems like so long ago, you know, because when I was asking her this it must have been 1908 or '9. I was just a little boy. I was a little boy and my Mama was working in the tobacco plant and my Mammy Ca'line took care of me and I took care of my brothers and my sister. My Daddy Genie was dead. He died young. He was my real Grandmother Lucy's boy and of course she was dead too. Her name was Lucille just like my sister and just like you. You named for Dahomey women, Lue."

∎

5

Pennsylvania seemed greener than Maryland did. It smelled like spring and even when we laughed at the Welcome to Pennsylvania sign we sniffed deeply the green spring smell. My brother said the only thing wrong with Pennsylvania was that it was full of Pennsylvanians and Fred grinned and then glanced into the rear-view mirror. Sammy and I looked behind us. There was a Pennsylvanian driving behind us, driving too close to our station wagon. A whiteboy driver in a cowboy hat driving a cowboy car and bent down low and stiff over the steering wheel. Sammy and I pointed at him and laughed loud and fell down all in the seat and the poor Pennsylvania whiteboy sat straight up and gunned around us three crazy spooks driving North and sped the hell in front of us and across the mountains scared and driving like hell. Like away from hell. Fred started to speed and we strained trying to catch up with him and laugh at him some more but we looked across every mountain and he was gone. We kept on, saying we were looking for our cowboy and followed the day across the Pennsylvania green until we left spring there in the high ground and the land turned slowly grey and hard and cracking and we were nearing New York State. The promised land.

■

6

"When Mammy Ca'line and them got to Virginia," my
Daddy would say, "the coffle was split up and she was sold to a
man named Bob Donald. Her brother was sold to somebody in
a close-by town and he was trained to be a blacksmith and her
sister was sold to a plantation next to Bob Donald's and
Mammy Ca'line got to see her sometime. Of course she never
saw her Mama again cause she was sold away. Mammy
Ca'line was eight years old. And I used to ask her, Mammy,
don't you wish you could have seen your Mama sometime?
And she would just shake her head. She never would say noth-
ing to me about her Mama but sometime when I was a boy I
would sit with her and Aunt Margaret Brown, who was her sis-
ter, while they rocked on the porch and I would hear them talk-
ing about do you remember different things. And they would
say about Do you remember Nat Turner's forays when we just
got here and Do you remember John Brown and the war be-
tween the states? And Mammy Ca'line would smile like at Aunt
Margaret Brown and say 'I'm glad you survived it, sister, and I
wonder what become of our Mama?' And they would just rock
and rock."

Smoke was hanging over Buffalo like judgment. We rode
silently through shortcuts we knew, and came at last into my
father's street. It was night. There were no children playing. In
the middle of the block the door to my father's house stood
open and lighted as it had when my mother had died. Fred
parked the car and we unstuck ourselves from the seats, tired
and limp from laughing. My husband and my brother took my
hands and we walked slowly toward the light, toward the fam-
ily we had tried to escape.

We are orphans, my brother whispered. Very softly.

■

lucy

I do not trouble my spirit to vindicate itself or be understood,
I see that the elementary laws never apologize.

—*Song of Myself*
Walt Whitman

1

"Lucille Sale, called Lucy, was the daughter of Caroline Donald and Sam Louis Sale," my Daddy would say. "They called him Uncle Louis like they did back then. This man, Bob Donald, bought Mammy Ca'line and set her to work in the orchard. They was big fruit growers and Ca'line worked in the orchards from when she was a little girl. One day when she had got big she was in the field and a carriage come by and stopped. And two old men was in it. It was Uncle Louis Sale and he was a slave but he was too old to work in the field and so his job was to drive his master in the carriage. His master was Old Man John F. Sale and he was a old man too, Lue, and blind. Uncle Louis had been given to his family as a boy. He was a present to their family. He was somebody and he was a present, a wedding present, Lue. And he was driving this carriage, an old man driving another old man, and he saw Ca'line in the orchard. And he stopped the horses and asked Old Man John F. to buy her for him for his wife. And Old Man John F. did. She was a young lady by then, Lue, and Uncle Louis had been born in 1777 but she was bought and went off to the Sale place and Old Man John F. married them legal cause he was a lawyer and they always said he was a good man. She lived there on the Sale place and they trained her to be a midwife and Mammy Ca'line and Uncle Louis had seven or more children, Lue, and one of the first ones was a girl. They called her Lucy but her name was Lucille. Like my own sister. And like you.

"Oh slavery, slavery," my Daddy would say. "It ain't something in a book, Lue. Even the good parts was awful."

■

2

My father looked like stone in a box. Like an old stone man caught in a box. He looks good, don't he, Lue? my sisters begged. Don't he look real good?

The room was heavy with flowers. My sisters had taken me to view the body and we were surrounded by cards bearing the names of my uncles and aunts and strange Polish names from our old neighborhood. I looked at the thin hook-nosed man in the box. He was still handsome, straight and military as he always was when he slept. He sleeps like he was dead, we used to laugh. His hand was curved as if his cane was in it, but his body was slightly on its side so that his missing leg was almost hidden. They were hiding his missing leg. The place where there was no leg was hidden. They were hiding his nothing. Nothing was hidden. They were missing nothing. I thought I was going to laugh. They were hiding where there was nothing to hide. Nothing was missing. I walked out of the room.

My father was an old man. My father had become an old man and I didn't even know it. This old man in a box was my father. Daddy had been an old man.

My sisters stood behind me. Don't he look good, Lue? They kept saying it. No, I finally answered. He's dead. I walked away.

My mother bore two children, a boy and a girl. My father was the father of four. He had three daughters by three different women, his first wife who died when she was twenty-one years old, my mother who triumphed with a son, and my youngest sister's mother who had been my father's lover when my mother was a bride. Our mothers had all known each other, had been friends. We were friends. My sisters and I. And my Mama had raised us all.

When Mama died they said he wouldn't last long. He'll have a hard time without Thel, they whispered, he can't make it without Thel. Even the widows and old girlfriends that gathered like birds nodded to each other. He needed Thel, he'll be gone soon.

But he fooled them. He was a strong man, a rock, and he lived on for ten years in his house, making a life. He took one of Mama's friends for his girlfriend, just as easily as he had married Mama when Edna Bell, his first wife and my sister Jo's mother, had died at twenty-one. And Mama's friend took care of him just as Mama had done, cooking and cleaning and being hollered at so much that once my children had asked me Is that lady Papa's maid or what? And I had answered No, not really, she's like my Mama was.

He lived on ten years in that house after Mama died, but my Mama lingered there too. His friend said she could hear her in the mornings early when it was time to get up and get his breakfast, and she would roll over and jump out of bed and run toward the kitchen, calling I'll get it, Thel, I'll get it. She was tough as a soldier, my father would say of my dead mother. She wasn't a Dahomey woman, but she was the Mama of one.

■

3

"When you was born we was going to name you Georgia," Daddy told me once. "Because my mother's name was Georgia and your Mama's mother was named Georgia too. But when I saw you there you was so pretty I told your Mama I wanted to name you Thelma for her. And she said she didn't like her name and for me to give you another name with the Thelma. So I looked at you and you looked just like one of us and I thought about what Mammy Ca'line used to say about Dahomey women and I thought this child is one of us and I named you Lucille with the Thelma. Just like my sister Lucille and just like my real Grandmother Lucy. Genie, my Daddy's mother. First Black woman legally hanged in the state of Virginia."

He said Black like that, back then. And he would be looking proud.

Fred and I slept in the room that had once been mine. We were going to find a motel, but my sisters cried and asked us to stay with them. Just one night, you'll just be one night, they said. You ought to stay. And I looked at them and knew that they were right. I ought to stay. My sisters had stood by my father's bed while his leg had been amputated and Jo had cursed the nurses and made them clean his mess in the hospital and my sister Punkin had held his hand and they had bought him his wheelchair. And you ought to stay, they said to Sammy and me.

Sammy grumbled and took his suitcase to his old room and went out to visit with his own children and to get drunk, and Fred took our bags up to my old room. I looked at the women who were my sisters, one seven years older than I, the other six months younger, and thought about the other death we had shared in this house. Mama. My Mama. Jo's mother had died in another town when Jo was a baby, and Punkin's mother was alive and cooking quietly at last in her lover's kitchen. Three women who had loved Daddy. Three daughters who had loved Daddy. I shook my head and walked up the stairs to my old room. These are my sisters, I whispered to myself.

Lue, Jo cried up the steps to me. We're scared. He's gonna haunt us.

No he won't. I tried to comfort.

He sure will haunt me, Jo was crying. I'm bad and he'll haunt me for sure.

Not you, Lue, Punkin whispered. He won't bother you. You always was his heart.

■

4

"They named his daughter Lucille," my Daddy would say. "They say she was a tall skinny dark-skinned girl, look just like her mother. Mammy Ca'line. They say they couldn't get her to work as hard as the rest and she was quiet and thought she was better than the rest. Mammy Ca'line taught her that, they say, and I wouldn't be surprised if she did. They tell me she was mean. Lucy was mean always, I heard Aunt Margaret Brown say to Mammy Ca'line one time. And Mammy just said no she wasn't mean, she was strong. 'Strong women and weak men,' is what she said, 'sister, we be strong women and weak men.' And I run up to her and said Mammy, I ain't weak. And she just smiled at me and said 'Not you, mister, you won't be weak. You be a Sayle.'

"And Mammy was a midwife all through the war and her daughter Lucy worked with her sometime and after the war, after emancipation like they said, they just kept up delivering babies all around, white and Black. And the town just grew up, after the war, Lue, cause a lot of white folks come South to make money you know, off the South's trouble. And one of them was a carpetbagger from Connecticut. Named Harvey Nichols. The white man Lucy killed."

I waited all night for morning. Fred and I lay without sleeping in the room that had been my own and cried and talked about my Daddy. He had been a great storyteller. His life had been full of days and his days had been full of life.

■

5

My father was born in Bedford Virginia in 1902. His father Gene Sayle had died when he was a little boy and his mother had gone to work in the tobacco factory, leaving my father and his two brothers and one sister in the care of her dead husband's grandmother. My father's great-grandmother, who had been a slave. My father had left school in the second or third grade and could barely write more than his name, but he was an avid reader. He loved books. He had changed his name to Sayles (instead of Sayle) after finding a part of a textbook in which the plural was explained. There will be more than one of me, my father thought, and he added the *s* to his name. He had worked in coal mines and in laboring camps throughout the South, and had come North during a strike at a steel plant which hired him. He had married as a young man a girl named Edna Bell who died at twenty-one and he had then married her friend Thelma Moore, who died at forty-four. I won't get married again, he used to say, I'm a jinx, to young women.

He and Edna Bell had had a daughter Josephine, called Jo. He and Thelma Moore had had a daughter Thelma Lucille and then a neighbor woman had borne him a daughter Elaine, called Punkin, six months later. Two years after, he and Thelma became the parents of a son. A son. He had no other children and he never slept with his wife again. He said he had seen his son ever since he was a little boy in Virginia and he had never wanted any other thing.

And now he was dead. Fred and I lay and listened to the house. My Daddy and Mama were dead and their house was full of them.

■

6

"Harvey Nichols was a white man," my Daddy would say,
"who come South after the war to make money. He brought his
wife and family down and bought himself a house and every-
thing. And it was close to the Sale place and all the slaves had
stayed there after emancipation because they said the Sales
was good people, but they had just changed their last name to
Sayle so people would know the difference. And this Harvey
Nichols saw Lucy and wanted her and I say she must have
wanted him too because like I told you, Lue, she was mean and
didn't do nothing she didn't want to do and nobody could force
her because she was Mammy Ca'line's child and everybody
round there respected Mammy Ca'line so much. And her
daughter Lucy had this baby boy by this Connecticut Yankee
named Harvey Nichols. They named the baby Gene Sayle. He
was my Daddy, Lue. Your own grandfather and Mammy
Ca'line's grandson. But oh, Lue, he was born with a withered
arm.

"Yes, Lord, he was born with a withered arm and when he
was still just a baby Lucy waited by the crossroad one night for
Harvey Nichols to come to her and when he rode up on a white
horse, she cocked up a rifle she had stole and shot him off his
horse and killed him, Lue. And she didn't run away, she didn't
run away, she waited right there by the body with the rifle in
her hand till the horse coming back empty-saddled to the sta-
ble brought a mob to see what had become of Harvey Nichols.
And when they got to the crossroad they found Lucy standing
there with the rifle in her hand. And they didn't lynch her, Lue,
cause she was Mammy Ca'line's child, and from Dahomey
women. That's what I believe. Mammy Ca'line got one of the
lawyer Sale family to defend her daughter, cause they was all
lawyers and preachers in that family. They had a legal trial and
Lucy was found guilty. And hanged. Mammy Ca'line took the
baby boy Genie and raised him and never let him forget who
he was. I used to ask her sometime, Mammy, was you scared

back then bout Granma Lucy? And she would look right at me and say 'I'm scared for you, mister, that's all.' She always called me mister. She said I was Mister Sayle. And Lue, I always was."

And Lucy was hanged. Was hanged, the lady whose name they gave me like a gift had her neck pulled up by a rope until the neck broke and I can see Mammy Ca'line standing straight as a soldier in green Virginia apart from the crowd of silent Black folk and white folk watching them and not the wooden frame swinging her child. And their shame making distance between them and her a real thing. And I know she made no sound but her mind closed around the picture like a frame and I know that her child made no sound and I turn in my chair and arch my back and make this sound for my two mothers and for all Dahomey women.

Later I would ask my father for proof. Where are the records, Daddy? I would ask. The time may not be right and it may just be a family legend or something. Somebody somewhere knows, he would say. And I would be dissatisfied and fuss with Fred about fact and proof and history until he told me one day not to worry, that even the lies are true. In history, even the lies are true.

And there would be days when we young Sayles would be trying to dance and sing in the house and Sammy would miss a step and not be able to keep up to the music and he would look over in the corner of the room and holler "Damn Harvey Nichols." And we would laugh.

■

gene

What is a man anyhow? what am I? what are you?

—Song of Myself
Walt Whitman

1

Daddy had surprised us and bought the house. Mama had thought he was throwing his money away, and would mumble about women being after him and him being bad after women, when one day he came home and threw a bankbook on the table, and some papers.

Every man has to do three things in life, he had said, plant a tree, own a house and have a son, and by God I've done two of them now. We had a house, he had bought a house and we were going to move. Punkin and Jo were married by then and I was soon going away to college. I was going to college. I had won a scholarship to Howard University and only Sammy would be at home. I was going away to college, a tall skinny kid who had never spent a night away from her Mama and now the daughters would all be gone and Daddy had bought a house.

He's getting old, Mama had whispered with great pride. She looked at him, glad that her time was coming. During the days that we were cleaning and packing and getting ready to move, Daddy would stop whatever he was doing and announce to us, I have had a son and now I own a house. All I got to do is plant a tree. And he would smile.

We children were not close to Daddy in those days. Punkin was walking the tight line stretched between her husband and her mother's children and us, her father's children, and she was quiet and withdrawn when we saw her. Jo had begun the slow dance between the streets and the cells that she practiced and practiced and Sammy had begun the young Black boy's initiation into wine and worse. And I had won a scholarship to Howard University. I was scared and proud and happy to get away. I had begun thinking of myself as special. Everybody said I was Daddy's favorite and I was the one who stayed with Mama and tried to watch out for her fits. I was a good girl. A smart girl. Lucille.

A week before we were to move I was to leave for Washington. The church gave a reception for me, the first person from our church to go to college, and everybody brought gifts and laughed and knew that I would make good. But I left Howard after two years. Lost my scholarship because I didn't study. I didn't have to, I thought. I didn't have to know about science and geography and things that I didn't want to know. I was a Dahomey woman. And so I came home to a disappointed and confused Mama and Daddy who was furious and defensive and sad.

Feet of clay, he said to me. My idol got feet of clay. God sent you to college to show me that you got feet of clay.

Daddy, I argued with him, I don't need that stuff, I'm going to write poems. I can do what I want to do! I'm from Dahomey women!

You don't even know where that is, he frowned at me. You don't even know what it means.

And I ran to my room and cried all night and waited for the day. Because he was right. I cried and cried and listened.

Again. The house was full of noise. Sammy coming in and Jo crying and pacing the floor and Punkin going to the bathroom and being sick. But I didn't hear my father and I listened all night. He won't haunt you, Lue, they had said. He was always crazy about you.

■

2

"My Daddy died before I was six," my Daddy would say. "One day I was playing in the field and Aunt Margaret Brown hollered out the window Hush up that noise, your Daddy is dead. I hollered back I don't care. Because I wanted to play.

"My Daddy's name was Genie and he had a withered arm. He was born with it, oh but Lue, he was a handsome man. Always wore a derby and he was the color brown of cinnamon and he had real light brown eyes. Oh he had these light brown eyes from his Daddy being a white man and after his Mama Lucy was dead Mammy Ca'line took him and raised him. And she spoiled him too, spoiled him so bad till he was wild. And the women was crazy about him. He was crazy bout them too, he had a whole lot of women, Lue, when I go back home everybody my age looks just like me. And wild! On holidays the sheriff used to come to Mammy Ca'line and ask her to please keep Genie at home so the town could have the holiday, but she wouldn't do it. No sir. 'He can go where he please,' she would say, 'he from Dahomey women.' And when the holiday come he would put on his derby hat and go out in the field and pile up his withered arm with bricks and walk straight down the Main Street of town breaking out store windows. But they wouldn't lock him up. Sometime they would wait till his arm was empty of bricks and then they would drive him back home to Mammy Ca'line. And she would just shake her head at him."

Daddy, we would laugh, your Daddy was a crazy man. We had us a crazy grandfather. And my father would sigh "No he wasn't crazy. He was just somebody whose Mama and Daddy was dead."

And we would say Oh Daddy he was too crazy, you had a crazy man for a Daddy.

And my father would say "No, he didn't hardly get to be a man. He wasn't much past thirty years old when he died."

∎

3

When I was born my father was thirty-five years old. The handsomest man in town, Mama always said. She was twenty-one, a plump brown girl who had never had a real boyfriend. He was always a wonder to her, like someone from a foreign place, and she would watch him and listen to his words as if they were commandments. He had been called Mr. Sayles Lord when he was young and thought he was some kind of a God man. Once I asked him why he was so sure that he was going to heaven. God knows me, he said. God understands a man like me. Mama didn't really understand such a man. But she loved him. She cleaned his mess and fed him and took his abuse and called him "your crazy Daddy" in a voice thick with love until the day she dropped dead at forty-four years old. And he lived on for ten years after. And missed her every day.

He would say that he could hear her in the house. And sometimes when he was coming home from work, he said that he could see her get up from the chair by the window and walk to the front door to meet him. And he could hear somebody soft saying Samuel. She never called him anything but Samuel. Because that's his name, she would say.

■

4

"Genie called me Rock," my Daddy would say, "and he would take me into all them old beer gardens and sit me up on a corner of the bar. Then he'd walk round the bar hollering to all the other men that I could whip their boys and he'd take bets on it. Some of them would run and get their sons and he'd lift me up when they came back and he'd laugh 'Down and get on em, Rock!' and I would jump from his arms and whip that other boy. Oh my Mama would be mad at him about that but she didn't never say anything to him about it. Her name was Georgia Hatcher and her family had belonged to the Lees. Genie was a barber at that time and he would go round to people's houses and cut their hair. First thing I ever remember is the sound of him coming home from cutting hair and singing at the top of his voice. Just singing as loud as he could. And my Mama would be just grinning cause he was so handsome and so wild. She didn't know I could see her but I remember her watching out for him and grinning, and Mammy Ca'line watching too and shaking her head and whispering Genie Genie Genie. We always been strong women and weak men, Lue, up till me.

"When my Daddy died I said I didn't care cause I wanted to play. And my Mama went to work in the tobacco plant and left us with Mammy Ca'line. After a little while my Mama married again. A man named Luke Stevens and, Lue, she had two more sons and a daughter. Mr. Luke was a good man, a real good man, but Mammy Ca'line spoiled us so, you know, and we treated him bad, we Sayles. She told us we didn't have to do what he said, you know. She shouldn't have told us that cause he was always good to us and he treated my Mama real good. But Mammy Ca'line would tell us that we was Sayle people and we didn't have to obey nobody. You a Sayle, she would say. You from Dahomey women.

"Only time I ever saw my Mama cry was she was sitting at the table reading a letter. It was night and the tobacco plant was laying off and so she was doing some day work and coming home to help Mammy Ca'line clean up after us at night. Some of her friends had gone off to New York City to look for work and they had wrote her a letter telling her to come too. But she had us kids, you know, and couldn't go. I asked her how come she wanted to go to New York City and she started crying and said 'I just want to see some things. I want to walk in the North and see some things.' Not long after that is when she married Mr. Luke. I asked Mammy Ca'line about why did my Mama want to see the North and everything. And she just looked at me. Then I asked her did she ever want to see some other place beside Virginia, and 'I already seen it, mister' is what she said."

■

5

After my mother was thirty-five years old she began having seizures. Epilepsy. Daddy was furious with her for having fits. For something happening that he couldn't understand and couldn't help. He would shout at her to stop sitting in that chair by the window, her chair. That chair is giving you fits, he would say. She went to clinics and took tests but she had the seizures regularly until she died. And after she was dead, my father began having them. Mild ones, not like my mother's, terrible to look at, but seizures all the same.

He had worked in a steel mill for over thirty years and had contracted emphysema. Emphysema and fits. And a brain tumor. He discovered he had a brain tumor during the course of a hospital stay because of the emphysema and the doctors wanted to operate. At first he refused. Nobody cuts my family, he insisted. But my sisters and my brother and I fussed and fussed until he finally agreed to it. They removed a tumor about the size of an orange from his brain and he was up and out of the hospital in a matter of weeks. And just the same. We saw no difference in him.

Later his leg died. Just shriveled up and turned black and died and the doctors said that they had to amputate it or the death would spread throughout his body. And so he let them cut it off and he got a cane. He would smile and point to the empty place. Yeah, they got my leg but they didn't get me, he would boast.

■

samuel

All goes onward and outward, nothing collapses,
And to die is different from what any one supposed, and luckier.

—*Song of Myself*
Walt Whitman

1

The morning of my father's funeral was grey and wet. Every-thing cried. Jo and Punkin and I stood waiting to be driven to the church in our stiff new black hats and veils. Sammy stood unsteady in the things that Fred had rushed out in the early morning rain and bought him. We were silent, a quiet place in the middle of girlfriends and cousins and my Aunt Lucille who had come from New Jersey in the night. She was standing as she always stood, stiff and military in the rain, surrounded by people who didn't like her. Daddy had loved his sister dearly and we resented his affection. She don't never call him, we would whisper, he always got to call her and she always want him to send for her. She don't even think about him and he crazy bout her.

She and I were in the first car and she turned to me when it came and took my arm. Lucille and Lucille. She was an old woman, an old soldier. I took her hand as we stepped into the car. I too was straight and quiet. Mammy Ca'line's great-grand-daughter and great-great-granddaughter. Dahomey women. We rode to the church in silence.

■

2

"The generations of Caroline Donald, born free among the Dahomey people in 1822 and died free in Bedford Virginia in 1910," my Daddy would say, "and Sam Louis Sale, born a slave in America in 1777 and died a slave in the same place in around 1860
are Dabney and Gabriel and Sam and Helen and John and Lucille,
called Lucy
who had a son named Gene by a man named Harvey Nichols
and then
she killed him,
and this boy Gene with a withered arm had three sons and a daughter
named Willie and Harvey and Samuel and Lucille
and Samuel who is me
named his boy Sam and
his daughter Lucille.
We fooled em, Lue, slavery was terrible but we fooled them old people. We come out of it better than they did."

■

3

My father was laid in the ground between his wives. The stones seemed strange to me. Edna Sayles. Thelma Sayles. I had never thought of Jo's mother as a Sayles before and the name seemed too big in my mouth. Punkin's mother waited, cooking at the house, and I thought of her and wondered where she would lie. My father was lowered into the ground between his wives and my face was wet before I realized it. I wanted to tell him something, my insides screamed. I remember everything. I believe. Everything shook and my Aunt Lucille was shaking my arm and crying. Crying without shame quietly and straight as a soldier. Mammy Mammy she was whispering in her tears, Mammy it's 1969, and we're still here. I held her hand tightly. Lucille and Lucille.

My father bumped against the earth. Like a rock.

■

thelma

They are alive and well somewhere,
The smallest sprout shows there is really no death,
And if ever there was, it led forward life, and does not wait at
   the end to arrest it,
And ceas'd the moment life appear'd.

—Song of Myself
Walt Whitman

Well,
my Mama was from Georgia. My Mama was born in Rome
Georgia in 1914. She used to tell us that she was from Rome,
and when we were little we thought she was Italian. But she
was a round brown lady from Georgia, and as Daddy said,
"Everybody from Georgia glad to be *from* there." Her father
had sent for her and her mother and sisters and brothers to
come to Depew after he had been North awhile. He had come
on the same train as my Daddy, in the strikebreaking. My
Daddy and my grandfather were friends and my Mama was
twelve years younger than my Daddy. My Daddy's first wife
was a good friend of my Mama and so was my little sister's
mother and so was his last girlfriend. All friends.

When the colored people came to Depew they came to be a
family. Everybody began to be related in thin ways that last and
last. The generations of white folks are just people but the gen-
erations of colored folks are families.

Depew is where I was born. Depew New York, in 1936.
Roosevelt time. It was a small town, mostly Polish, all its life
turned like a machine around the steel mill. We lived in a
house on Muskingum Street, and my Mama's family lived on
Laverack. My grandparents lived in this big frame house on
Laverack Street with one toilet. And in that house were my
Mama's family, the Moores, and a lot of other people, lines of
people, old and young.

There was an old man who was a deacon, a pillar of the
church. I remember once in prayer meeting, he was praying
and the lights went out . . . a blackout, you know, in the second
world war. And he was deep in the middle of his best praying.
He was a very religious man, a deacon, and all of a sudden the
lights went out and he looked up and shouted "Dammit, now,
God!" then went on with his prayer. A good prayer too.

Our whole family lived there. In Depew. All the Moores, I
mean. All around the steel mill. My grandfather and Daddy
and uncles and all our men. Turning around the plant.

Depew. One of the earliest things I remember was the goat in the backyard. Our house was on top of a big hill and across the yard and down the hill in the back were the Moores. And Grandma kept a goat back there. Depew.

The closest big city was Buffalo, twelve miles away. One time daddy walked there to buy a dining room set. He was the first colored man in Depew to have a dining room set. And he walked to Buffalo to get it. He got it on credit from Peoples', a store where they gave colored people credit back then. This is what it was like: you got this credit from Peoples' store and the Peoples' man would come around to your house every week and collect. It would just be fifty cents or a dollar, but that was some money in those times and you know it went on for so long. So long. My Daddy paid something to the Peoples' man for as long as I can remember. Me and my brother used to hate him because he would come over every Saturday and collect and Daddy called him Mr. Pitterman but he called Daddy Sam. And his name was Samuel too, Samuel Pitterman, and if Daddy could be called Sam so could he. But he never was. Every Saturday he would come over and even after we moved to Buffalo when I was five or six, he would collect and then he would sit with Daddy on the porch and they would talk over old days. And Daddy would look forward to it.

He used to carry merchandise in the trunk of his car, Sam Pitterman, and he would sell things out of it. One Christmas he gave me and Punkin matching white crepe skirts, pleated all around. We put them in the bottom drawer of our dresser where the mice had gnawed and left them there.

Anyway, my Daddy wanted to have this dining room set and he walked to Buffalo to get it and when he got to Peoples' the salesman there told him he didn't need a dining room set. And Daddy told the man that his great-grandmother was a Dahomey woman and he could have anything he wanted. And so he got it. And walked back home, and they delivered the set. First colored man to own a dining room set in Depew New York.

Roosevelt time. War time.

I remember when my uncle came home from the second world war, my Mama's baby brother. He belonged to the ninety-second division, which was the colored infantry, I think, and they had been in Italy. Oh we were all so proud of him, and one afternoon my Grandma was sitting by the window looking out, and my aunt came into the kitchen from getting the mail and said "Mother, we got a letter from Buddy . . . and Here It Is!" And my uncle come grinning through the door with his soldier's suit on and oh my Grandma Moore laughed and cried and laughed again. I always remember how my Grandma Moore just sang out "Oh here's my Buddy Buddy Buddy Buddy!"

She was my grandmother that called me Genius. My Mama's mother. The Moores moved to Buffalo a while after we did, and they moved to downtown. She believed that I was twelve years old until the day she died, and I was married and pregnant. Always thought I was twelve, and she called me Genius because she knew I went to college.

When I went away to college, well, that was some time. People couldn't get it straight that I was going to Howard and not Harvard. Nobody in our family had graduated from high school at that time, and at that time no member of our church had ever gone to college. I had won this scholarship, you know, and they gave me this big party at the church. The Baptist church.

Now we didn't know a thing about going to college. I remember I took my Grandma's wedding trunk, all held together with rope. Me and Mama went over to Peoples' and bought me a black silk skirt and a red see-through blouse and we packed Grandma Moore's wedding trunk. When they delivered it at Howard, all those ritzy girls from Chicago and Texas, oh I was so embarrasssed I went down at night to pick it up. This old trunk with thick rope around it and Georgia Moore written in ink. Anyway, I went away to college, and before I left I had to go and say goodby to everybody.

And we went to see Grandma and she was watching for us, and when we started down her block, she ran out on the porch hollering "Everybody, Everybody, Here come my Genius!" And all her neighbor people come running out on the porch. And here I come, here I come.

My Grandma Moore told me to behave myself away from home, and I promised that I would. I had never been away from home and my own people before and let me tell you I was scared but I didn't let on. Then she asked me "Where was Moses when the lights went out?" and I said "Grandma, I just don't know," and she said "Well, that's all right, just keep your dress tail down," and I said "Yes, ma'am," because I understood that part.

There was another old lady, older than Grandma, named Miss Washington, and she had been born in slavery. I went to see her and she gave me these doilies, all these doilies she had crocheted with her own hands. She told me about when she was a tiny girl and Mr. Lincoln had come by in a parade and her mother had picked her up and made her wave her hand. She told me about this proud thing and gave me these doilies to take to college, and I went off to school.

I was sixteen years old and went away to college and I had never slept a night away from my Mama and when me and my friend Retha and my friend Betty got to Washington they had this huge train station. I had never seen a place like that and I started to almost cry and I said to Retha that as soon as I ate I was going back home. Then a Howard man came up to us and looked at Betty all little and cute with her college clothes and her name tag on and said "You'll love it here, and we'll love you," and he turned to me and asked me if I was her mother. From that moment I knew I wouldn't last. And I didn't. Two years. That was all.

But what a two years it was! What a time! I was from New York, so that was a big deal, and I was a drama major, so that was a big deal too. At that time, at Howard, if you weren't light-skinned or had long hair you had to have something pretty strong going for you. Well, I was a drama major from New York. They didn't know that Buffalo is a long way from New York City, and for them that did know, I could lay claim to Canada, so it worked out well enough.

My Daddy wrote me a letter my first week there, and my Daddy could only write his name. But he got this letter together and it said "Dear Lucilleman, I miss you so much but you are there getting what we want you to have be a good girl signed your daddy." I cried and cried because it was the greatest letter I ever read or read about in my whole life. Mama wrote me too and her letter said, "Your daddy has written you a letter and he worked all day."

Being away from home, I didn't even know how to do it. I used to think I was going to starve to death. Nobody had any notion of what I needed or anything. One time Mama sent me a box full of tuna fish. I hid it under my bed and at night I would take it out and open can after can of tuna fish. And I was always afraid I'd make a mistake and Daddy would find out. I knew he'd know whatever I did. Whatever I did. But I was proud. The first Thanksgiving I went back home and now I had only been gone since September but when I stepped off the train Daddy and my sister Jo were there and Jo said "Oh, she don't look so different," but I started talking with a Washington accent and I even had to try to remember the way home. I was a mess. I thought everything seemed so little.

When we moved to Buffalo, we were moving to the big city. I was six or seven, maybe even five, and we moved to Buffalo one night in a truck. We thought it was the biggest place in the world. The lady who owned the house had left a doll for me in the attic, and that doll and that attic and that whole house smelled like new days. Purdy Street.

My Daddy was from Bedford Virginia and he left home when he was a boy and did a lot of moving around. He was so handsome they called him Mr. Sayles Lord, and when he'd walk down the street women would come out of their houses and say it. He used to go to dances and sometimes in the middle of a dance he would get tired and throw his hat down and shout The Dance Is Over, and all the people would stop playing music and dancing and go home.

He came to Depew when a train came through the South offering colored men jobs and a trip North. And he got on in Virginia and my Grandpa Moore had got on in Georgia. When my Daddy got North he worked in the plant and he married Edna Bell, my sister Jo's mother, who died when she was only twenty-one years old. He used to say that they didn't know why she died until one night she came to him in a dream and told him to have them check her for consumption because that's what she had. And they checked and found it. Tuberculosis. Consumption.

TB. You know just a few of us in our family have never had TB. I never had it. Some people had it twice. I never had it, and my cousins used to say it was because I was a good girl.

When I was a girl if my cousins would curse around me they would always say "Excuse me, Lucille." They would never say anything about anything around me and that's why there were all patches of things I learned late. I had a girlfriend who used to talk to me about dope though. Before I went away to school she was walking the street, and she took me up to where she stayed with this man who was a pimp, and they had a list of places in Washington D.C. where they said they better not hear about me going. They didn't want me to disgrace them in Washington D.C. I paid attention, too, because I always wanted to do the right thing. I always wanted to.

I have two sisters, half-sisters, and a brother. I used to be a little bit scared of my older sister Jo. She's getting older now, though, and she's playing mother to her kids and grandmother to their kids in a big way. Last time I saw her she was standing on Daddy's porch with her arm around her boyfriend Bobby and he was waving. Bobby, her boyfriend, only had one eye. She had another boyfriend with one eye once and I heard Daddy say to himself one time "All her men just got one eye, can't she get a man got two good eyes?"

There were a lot of small-time folks like that in Buffalo. Lot of very nice people who were also small-time crooks mostly because there wasn't much else to be. Just about everybody was on the welfare, giving up a little bit of everything to get on the city. A little bit of everything and a whole lot of pride. There was an older colored lady that was a caseworker and everybody hated to see her coming she was so mean. Mama and Daddy never were on the welfare and it made us proud. They made us proud, wanted us to be.

A lady down the street from us had a civil service job, just nothing, just a file clerk or like that, but Daddy used to tell me when she would pass by "Lue, you keep being a good girl and keep your grades good and you can be just like her." She married a man who was a chiropractor and published a little newspaper. He also had a shoe repair shop and he used to fix the shoes himself. He would be in there late at night tacking shoes together with a tack hammer. His shop was across the street from where we lived, next-door to the grocery shop owned by two white women from Canada. They used to sue Mama all the time because she would get credit and get credit without telling Daddy and not pay it back and finally they would sue her. They would send summonses to the house. They used to always tell me to get away, get away, and want to take me to Canada for a while. They thought I seemed like a nervous child.

I seemed a lot of things. I used to go to the blackmarket meat store during the war and it was always packed and I would lean on the counter and it seemed like I was going to faint and they would always wait on me before it was really my turn. I seemed a lot of things.

One time Mama bought herself a wedding ring set and of

course she couldn't pay for it. She must have known that. But she had said to me once that I should always try to have some-thing I could pawn, and anyway she had never had a wedding ring, so she bought these rings. When they were going to sue her she sent me, a small child too, downtown to take them back and to tell the jeweler that I was the lady next-door's little girl and Mrs. Sayles said she was returning the rings. He must have seen through that, but he didn't let on.

Oh she made magic, she was a magic woman, my Mama. She was not wise in the world but she had magic wisdom. She was twenty-one years old when she got married but she had had to stay home and help take care of her brothers and sisters. And she had married Daddy right out of her mother's house. Just stayed home, then married Daddy who had been her friend Edna Bell's husband after Edna Bell died. She never went out much. She used to sit and hum in this chair by the window. After my brother was born, she never slept with my Daddy again. She never slept with anybody, for twenty years. She used to tell me "Get away, get away. I have not had a normal life. I want you to have a natural life. I want you to get away."

A lot of people were always telling me to get away.

She used to sit in this chair by the window and hum and rock. Some Sundays in the summertime me and her used to go for walks over to the white folks section to look in their windows and I would tell her when I grew up I was going to take her to a new place and buy her all those things.

Once in a while we would go to the movies, me and her. But after she started having her fits I would worry her so much with Are you all right Ma and How do you feel Ma that we didn't go as often. Once I asked her if she was all right and she said she would be fine if I would leave her alone.

Mostly on Friday nights when Daddy had gone out and the other kids had gone out too we would get hamburgers and pop from the store and sit together and after we got TV we would watch TV. On New Year's Eve we would wait up until mid-night and I would play Auld Lang Syne on the piano while me and my Mama sang and then we would go to bed.

Oh she was magic. If there were locks that were locked tight, she could get a little thing and open them. She could take old bent hangers and rags and make curtains and hang drapes. She ironed on chairs and made cakes every week and everybody loved her. Everybody.

When Daddy bought the house away from Purdy Street, Mama didn't know that he had been saving his money. One day he just took us to see this house he was buying. I was going away to college that fall and Punkin was off and married and we were scattering but he had bought us this house to be together in. Because we were his family and he loved us and wanted us to be together. He was a strong man, a strong family man, my Daddy. So many people knew him for a man in a time when it wasn't so common. And he lived with us, our Daddy lived in our house with us, and that wasn't common then either. He was not a common man. Now, he did some things, he did some things, but he always loved his family.

He hurt us all a lot and we hurt him a lot, the way people who love each other do, you know. I probably am better off than any of us, better off in my mind, you know, and I credit Fred for that. Punkin she has a hard time living in the world and so does my brother and Jo has a hard time and gives one too. And a lot of all that is his fault, has something to do with him.

And Mama, Mama's life was—seemed like—the biggest waste in the world to me, but now I don't know, I'm not sure any more. She married him when she was a young twenty-one and he was the only man she ever knew and he was the only man she ever loved and how she loved him! She adored him. He'd stay out all night and in the morning when he came home he'd be swinging down the street and she would look out the window and she'd say loud "Here come your crazy Daddy." And the relief and joy would make her face shine. She used to get up at five every morning to fix his breakfast for him and she one time fell down the back steps and broke her ankle and didn't see about it until after she had fixed breakfast, had gotten back up the steps and finished.

She would leave him. She would leave him and come in every morning at five o'clock to fix his breakfast because "your Daddy works hard," she would fuss, "you know you can't fix him a decent meal."

She would sit in the movies. She would leave him and sit in the movies and I would see her there and try to talk and make things right. I always felt that I was supposed to make things right, only I didn't know how, I didn't know how. I used to laugh and laugh at the dinner table till they thought I was crazy but I was so anxious to make things right.

I never knew what to do. One time they were arguing about something and he was going to hit her and my sister Punkin, who had a different mother, she ran and got the broom and kept shouting "If you hit Mama I'll kill you" at Daddy. My brother and I didn't do anything but stand there and it was our Mama but we didn't do anything because we didn't know what to do.

Another time they were arguing and I was in the kitchen washing dishes and all of a sudden I heard my Mama start screaming and fall down on the floor and I ran into the room and she was rolling on the floor and Daddy hadn't touched her, she had just started screaming and rolling on the floor. "What have you done to her," I hollered. Then "What should I do, what should I do?" And Daddy said "I don't know, I don't know, I don't know, she's crazy," and went out. When he left, Mama lay still, and then sat up and leaned on me and whispered "Lue, I'm just tired, I'm just tired."

The last time ever I saw her alive she had been undergoing tests to find out what caused her epilepsy and I leaned over to kiss her and she looked at me and said "The doctors took a test and they say I'm not crazy. Tell your Daddy."

I wanted to make things better. I used to lay in bed at night and listen for her fits. And earlier than that, when I was younger, a little girl, I would lay awake and listen for their fights. One night they were shouting at each other and my sister Punkin whispered out of her stillness "Lue, are you awake?" "No," I mumbled. She stirred a little. "That's good," she said.

I wanted to make things right. I always thought I was supposed to. As if there was a right. As if I knew what right was. As if I knew.

My Mama dropped dead in a hospital hall one month before my first child was born. She had gone to take a series of tests to try to find out the cause of her epilepsy. I went to visit her every day and we laughed and talked about the baby coming. Her first grandchild. On this day, Friday, February 13, it was raining but I started out early because I had not gone to see her the day before. My aunt and my Uncle Buddy were standing in the reception area and as I came in they rushed to me saying "Wait, Lue, wait, it's not visiting hours yet." After a few minutes I noticed other people going on toward the wards and I started up when my aunt said "Where you going, Lue?" and I said "Up to see my Mama," and they said all together "Lue Lue your Mama's dead." I stopped. I said "That's not funny." Nobody laughed, just looked at me, and I fell, big as a house with my baby, back into the telephone booth, crying "Oh Buddy Oh Buddy, Buddy, Buddy."

One month and ten days later another Dahomey woman was born, but this one was mixed with magic.

Things don't fall apart. Things hold. Lines connect in thin ways that last and last and lives become generations made out of pictures and words just kept. "We come out of it better than they did, Lue," my Daddy said, and I watch my six children and know we did. They walk with confidence through the world, free sons and daughters of free folk, for my Mama told me that slavery was a temporary thing, mostly we was free and she was right. And she smiled when she said it and Daddy smiled too and saw that my sons are as strong as my daughters and it had been made right.

And I could tell you about things we been through, some awful ones, some wonderful, but I know that the things that make us are more than that, our lives are more than the days in them, our lives are our line and we go on. I type that and I swear I can see Ca'line standing in the green of Virginia, in the green of Afrika, and I swear she makes no sound but she nods her head and smiles.

The generations of Caroline Donald born in Afrika in 1823 and Sam Louis Sale born in America in 1777 are
Lucille
who had a son named
Genie
who had a son named
Samuel
who married
Thelma Moore and the blood became Magic and their daughter is
Thelma Lucille
who married Fred Clifton and the blood became whole and their children are
Sidney
Fredrica
Gillian
Alexia   four daughters and
Channing
Graham   two sons,
and the line goes on.
"Don't you worry, mister, don't you worry."

∎

Backward I see in my own days where I sweated through fog with linguists and contenders,
I have no mockings or arguments, I witness and wait.

—*Song of Myself*
Walt Whitman

about the author

Lucille Clifton was born in Depew, New York, and educated at the State University of New York at Fredonia and Howard University. She has taught at Coppin State College, Goucher College, and the American University in Washington, D.C. Her other teaching experiences have included appointments as Elliston Poet at the University of Cincinnati, Jenny Moore Visiting Lecturer in Creative Writing at George Washington University, and Woodrow Wilson Scholar at Fisk University, Trinity College and other universities. She currently teaches at the University of California at Santa Cruz. Clifton's awards and distinctions as a poet and fiction writer include The University of Massachusetts Press' Juniper Prize for poetry, a nomination for the Pulitzer Prize in poetry, an Emmy Award from the American Academy of Television Arts and Sciences, creative writing fellowships from the National Endowment for the Arts and Poet Laureate of the State of Maryland.

∎

BOA EDITIONS, LTD.
AMERICAN POETS CONTINUUM SERIES